10 Years, 13 Seconds: The Conor McGregor Story

SEAN BLACK

.

ISBN: 1530021081
ISBN-13: 978-1530021086

AUTHOR'S NOTE

This short volume is intended to give the general reader a broad overview of Ireland's newest world champion, and cultural phenomenon, Conor McGregor.

If you are an avid devotee of mixed martial arts (MMA), or have, like so many people in Ireland, and around the world, been following every single step of Conor McGregor's journey from Dublin to Las Vegas, you may wish to wait for a more comprehensive study of his career.

Both McGregor himself and his coach John Kavanagh have books slated to appear in the not too distant future. Kavanagh's book in particular promises to be a fascinating read. In a sport full of big characters, none bigger than McGregor, John Kavanagh's own story is arguably more compelling than many of the fighters.

In the meantime, if you'd like to know more about Conor McGregor, and how he got from there to here, or you'd just like to know what all the fuss surrounding MMA and the UFC is then this introductory volume may be a good place to start.

PREFACE

I earn my living writing novels. More precisely, I write thrillers. Action, suspense and tension are what make a reader turn the pages. But what brings them back are characters. Very often one character. A hero. A villain. Someone who may only appear in a handful of chapters, but who ends up stealing the show.

Characters that live long in the mind share one quality above all others. They are compelling. They stay with you. You may love them. You may hate them. You may laugh at them. It really doesn't matter which. The only thing that counts is that they hold your attention.

In early 2015, I chanced upon an interview with a young Irish MMA fighter by the name of Conor McGregor. Traveling by train into my office in Dublin every day I had heard the name in numerous conversations, mostly, but not exclusively, among young men. He wasn't always talked about in the most flattering of terms. Ireland can be the land of a thousand welcomes and as many begrudgers. But he was being talked about. A lot. And, as the old saying goes, the only thing worse than being talked about is not being talked about.

Something was going on. At the very least there was a ripple in the force field of a popular culture that has become dominated by people who are famous for being famous. Make a sex tape. Be an idiot on reality TV; the stupider, the better. Behead innocent aid workers and post it on social media. Hey presto, instant fame.

This was different. Qualitatively different. Conor McGregor was becoming famous for actually doing something.

That something, those seconds, or minutes, in the Octagon, demanded hours of practice every day. They demanded dedication. Discipline. Sacrifice. They demanded all he had. Then they demanded things he likely hadn't realized he did have.

I can't remember the precise details of the video interview I watched on the homepage of *The Irish Independent* back in early 2015. But I do recall spending the rest of the day, and most of the following day playing catch up on the Conor McGregor phenomenon. And, even to the untrained eye, it was very obvious that he was a very special individual. A once in a generation character who combined tremendous showmanship with great ability, almost superhuman drive, and the sharpest of minds.

No fighter, of whatever variety, has proven quite this compelling since Muhammad Ali. That's not to say that Conor McGregor is an equivalent figure. Cassius Clay begat Ali, a man who refused to fight in Vietnam and converted to Islam, and thus earned a much deeper, more concrete place in world culture and history than any sportsman likely ever will.

However is is possible to argue that since Ali, no sporting figure, and particularly no pugilist, has possessed the qualities of athletic prowess, articulacy, and fierce intelligence that Conor

McGregor has. Put simply, McGregor is a transcendent figure whose reach extends far beyond MMA.

At times Muhammad Ali raised boxing to the level of an art form. McGregor, with his fascination with movement can be said to do the same. With both men, there is beauty within the brutality of their trade. But there is more than the ability to out think, out move, and out fight an opponent. There is a lot more.

While numerous journalists have focused on McGregor's ability to talk up a fight, and deliver memorable, and often funny quotes, that is perhaps a superficial point of comparison. McGregor, like Ali, is a master of psychological warfare; of baiting, riling, and plain undermining his opponent before they square up. Sure, many fighters, and other sports people, indulge in trash talk. But McGregor, like Ali before him, goes beyond that. He studies. He probes. He dissects. He locates an opponent's emotional hot spots, and psychological vulnerabilities, and in press conferences and via social media, is unrelenting in targeting them.

It may be going too far to say that McGregor has already beaten his opponents before they even step into the Octagon to fight him. After all, there is still the physical work to be done. However, it's clear to see that they often arrive in a less than optimal psychological state.

If fighting, like gambling, is about finding an edge, the war of words that takes place before a fight often provides McGregor with an opportunity to lay the groundwork for victory; to establish an advantage by unsettling the person they have been matched against. Opponents can claim to have shrugged it off. They can tell reporters that it's had no impact. And they can mean it. They can believe it. The problem is that the human mind doesn't work like that. Below the level of conscious thought lies the subconscious. That is where the seeds of doubt can take root. In a highly pressurised situation such as a mixed martial arts contest, even the slightest glimmer of uncertainty can prove fatal.

McGregor's forensic dissection goes beyond the study of his opponent's psyche. It extends to their physical state and fighting style. Because MMA integrates a range of fighting disciplines, there is more to study. Different fighters come to MMA from different backgrounds. Some have started out as boxers, others come from wrestling, kick boxing, Brazilian jiu jitsu (BJJ), or any number of other martial arts. The permutations are vastly greater than boxing. The calculations that have to be made are greater. There is a greater risk of making an error when it comes to strategy and training.

MMA is, by definition, more complex and more intellectually challenging, than boxing. It makes a greater range of demands on a fighter. Both sports can be brutal, but MMA not only allows, but demands that fighters pursue their opponents to the ground. It's often these exchanges, with both fighters on the ground, that lead the sport's detractors to label it as unnecessarily violent.

Violent or not, what happens when you strip away the bravado, and the hype surrounding McGregor's ascent? Study his work, both within and without the Octagon, and it very quickly becomes clear that he is a singular, and singularly talented athlete, who is worthy of serious study.

Dana White, the public face of MMA's premier promotional organisation, the UFC (Ultimate Fighting Championship), has whimsically likened McGregor to the Notre Dame football mascot; a ginger bearded, barrel chested, Irish leprechaun that carries more than a hint of swagger. He has a point. The likeness is there, and being Irish has proved a key component of Brand McGregor in America.

However, while McGregor can appear cartoonish, he is far from a cartoon. He is a young man of fierce intelligence. It can be glimpsed in between the trash talk and the endless grind of promotion. A PR treadmill that seems at times, and surely is, far more draining to him than any number of training sessions and rounds of sparring. Yet he knows that promotion and marketing are an essential part of the fight game.

Inside and outside the Octagon, Conor McGregor seems to grasp every aspect of the business he is engaged in. He is the complete package. A fighter. A showman. And now, an undisputed world champion. Yet this is likely only the end of the beginning when it comes to his story. A story that in professional terms started a decade ago on the north side of Dublin.

Sean Black
Dublin, Ireland
December 13th, 2015

10 YEARS, 13 SECONDS

There is a saying that's popular among movie industry insiders in Los Angeles: it takes ten years to become an overnight success.

While the idea of overnight success makes for great newspaper copy, it rarely stands up to even the barest of scrutiny. Success is rarely magically bestowed. Even with talent, it takes hard work, determination, and the ability to deal with set backs, and rejection. The idea of an effortless ascent to fame and fortune is seductive. It's also, as many find to their cost, an illusion.

27-year-old Dublin native, Conor McGregor, is an overnight success who has been ten years in the making. Or, more precisely, ten years and thirteen seconds. The thirteen seconds are what screenwriters call the hook. But going in, anyone attempting to understand McGregor's story has to acknowledge that it was the ten years of hard work that made those mesmerising thirteen seconds the world witnessed on December 12th, 2015 at the MGM Grand arena in Las Vegas possible.

No ten years? No thirteen seconds. But before we get to the ten years, and the time before that, what about those thirteen seconds?

MGM Grand
Las Vegas, Nevada
December 12th, 2015

Like some marauding Mongol horde, or longship fleet of plundering Viking berkserkers, the Irish have invaded Las Vegas; invaded and taken over. Over nine thousand of them, almost all young, working class and male have made the five thousand mile journey from Ireland to Las Vegas, Nevada. They are here to see Conor McGregor fight reigning world champion, Brazilian Jose Aldo, for the UFC featherweight championship. It's a contest that had been due to take place in the summer, but had been postponed due to Aldo being injured.

In his stead, Chad Mendes, a thirty-year-old American wrestler turned MMA fighter, had stepped in to fight McGregor. McGregor won, becoming the interim champion. The bout with Jose Aldo was re-scheduled. In the days and hours before the contest, McGregor, who was been the bookies' favorite begins to drift in the market. The money, the late money, and therefore the smart money (or so the orthodoxy goes) is coming for Aldo. By the day of the fight, the odds are even. It's simply too close to call.

Even McGregor's most fervent fans will, in their more private moments, admit to being nervous about how their man will do. McGregor is a phenomenon with the record to go with it. But Aldo has been champion for ten years. Aldo is a fighter whose gritty demeanor was forged by a childhood growing up in hardscrabble poverty in Brazil.

The stakes are high. Many, both in Brazil, and

to a lesser but noticeable degree back home in Ireland, would like nothing more than to see McGregor taken down a peg or two. There is talk of McGregor having been groomed for success by the UFC who see in him a one-man publicity and cash generating machine who stands in stark contrast to the taciturn Aldo who requires a translator (a definite minus point in an American market where the media have lapped up McGregor's every utterance).

In the very eye of the storm, perfectly calm, almost supernaturally composed, stands McGregor. As he has so many times before, he has already told everyone the method of victory, and the round. A win by knockout. In the first.

His previous predictions have been eerily accurate, and yet. . .

The mood on the day of the fight is loud, and boisterous, but also strangely businesslike. Everyone has waited long enough for these two men to meet and settle matters. The commentators, the crowd, the millions watching on TV and via the internet (and paying handsomely for the privilege) are primed and ready.

Knife edge.

Too close to call.

No clear favorite.

All these terms apply as McGregor and his team leave the dressing room and make their way out into the arena. They walk through a sea of Irish flags towards the cage. McGregor appears, as he always does, a picture of supreme composure. In contrast to the crowd's fevered excitement and cries of *Ole! Ole! Ole!* (currently enjoying a resurgence as Ireland's unofficial national anthem), he seems positively serene, as casual as any man on his way to work at a job that he enjoys and knows he does well.

Many fighters proclaim victory before the event. None do it with such certainty that they seem to conjure up the age-old debate over whether our lives are already pre-destined. McGregor's composure goes beyond a lack of nerves, or the will to win. He already knows what will happen. If congruence, the ability to align your beliefs, your physical state and your true nature is the key to success then perhaps all that does matter is showing up.

Inside the MGM Grand Arena the lights dim as the plaintive strains of The Foggy Dew, an Irish folk song with a deep resonance for the Irish plays. Emerging into the tunnel, the music switches up and McGregor begins his walkout. He acknowledges the crowd, a few lucky fans get a high five, but even with his team around him and thousands of cheering fans willing him on, the fighter's walk is a lonely one. Not that you would know it from the way McGregor mugs for the camera, and bounces Tigger-like towards the Octagon.

Hugs for his team, a quick check over by UFC officials, a brief two-arms raised acknowledgement of the crowd, and he's up and then inside the Octagon. Inside his place of work, an eight-sided steel cage, he doesn't so much limber up as prowl.

The crowd in the arena and those watching around the world, glimpse the man fascinated by movement as he plants his legs, squats and stretches. He throws a perfect spinning kick into the air. Beyond the grace of his movement there appears to be something akin to joy, or at the very least, freedom.

By contrast, Aldo makes his entrance to boos from the crowd and more shouts of Ole! Ole! Ole! from the traveling Irish fans. It's easy to read too much into his body language after the event, but the contrast between his and McGregor's demeanor is pronounced. Maybe he is simply focussed, but for focussed you could also read tense.

Only Jose Aldo truly knows what his state of mind is and the degree to which the crowd is getting to him. He has been a proud, and honorable champion, so perhaps the lack of respect he's being shown unsettles him fractionally. Or perhaps none of it even registers. Even champions can expect a hostile reaction from sections of a crowd once in a while.

Once inside the Octagon, Aldo's gaze isn't out into the crowd. It's down towards the canvas. Later, the Monday morning quarterbacks will claim it shows nerves. Others will point out that Aldo's body language is no different than it normally is before a fight. He is not the showman that McGregor is. He hasn't had to be. He does his talking in the Octagon with his fists and feet. Quiet, introverted, he can appear like the anti-McGregor. The number one pound for pound fighter in the UFC, Aldo has not lost a fight in over a decade and has seven consecutive successful defenses of his title before tonight.

As the announcer introduces the main event, it is hard to hear him above the singing of the Irish fans. The atmosphere is nearing fever pitch.

The referee calls the two men into the center of the Octagon. He gives his instructions. He concludes by telling them that if they wish to touch gloves (a sign of respect between fighters) they may do so now. Neither man does.

McGregor and Aldo retreat to opposite sides of the Octagon. While McGregor hunkers, squats and sways, the picture of relaxation as he talks to Aldo, Aldo stands, right fist raised, left arm swaying, looking as tense and uptight as McGregor is loose.

The referee signals for the fight to start. McGregor almost prances forward. His movement at times appears comical to the untrained eye. What is supposed to be a closely contested, grueling contest between two evenly matched fighters has begun. The crowd are settling into their seats, getting comfy, eyes flitting between the Octagon and the view offered by the big screens. No one has anticipated what happens next. Or if they did anticipate the match of fighting styles, and McGregor's tactical approach, they certainly could not have anticipated such a short contest.

McGregor has moved forward, meeting his opponent in the middle of the Octagon. With his chin jutting forward, and arm reached outed, McGregor puts the first pressure on Aldo. He quickly claims ground before just as quickly retreating back. No punches or kicks thrown as yet, this is the physical manifestation of the psychological aspect of MMA fighting. Movement, occupation of space, the kicks and punches that are not delivered, these are all part of the three-dimensional game of chess that makes the sport so fascinating.

McGregor throws the first punch. A long left straight hand. He immediately ducks as Aldo counters with a left hook. McGregor bounces back. There is a broad smile on his face. Neither man has landed a blow on the other, but McGregor seems happy to have tested a hypothesis about how Aldo would fight and found it has held good.

Next McGregor throws an oblique kick towards Aldo's leading leg. Again this is tactical. It's a move designed not to hurt Aldo so much as ensure that McGregor can place his right leg where he needs it to be in order to deliver his trademark left hand.

Faking to throw a right hand punch, Aldo launches forward with his left. As Aldo throws the punch, lunging forward to generate power, McGregor's left counter punch is already on its way. McGregor's timing is immaculate. His left hand connects perfectly to Aldo's chin.

A freeze frame shows Aldo's face distorted by the force of the blow, his eyes shut. He goes down, falling to the canvas. Being MMA rather than boxing, McGregor follows Aldo down, launching a couple of quick hammer blows to Aldo's head before the referee, moving as fast as he can, pushes McGregor away and stops the contest.

While McGregor races across to climb atop the

Octagon there is a brief moment of shocked disbelief. The action itself has been a blur. McGregor's punch was so fast, and so perfectly timed and delivered, it appears almost cartoonish when viewed live and without the benefit of slow motion. It is as if McGregor is running at 24 frames per second while everyone else lags behind. There is a disconnect between what the crowd just witnessed and their ability to process it.

Even McGregor's coach, John Kavanagh, who has trained McGregor for over a decade, seems momentarily taken aback by how quickly and decisively the contest has been concluded.

The palpable shock is soon replaced by sheer elation. It is a moment of pure victory of the kind that life rarely, and for most people, never, delivers. Over ten years of hard, unrelenting work has paid off in just thirteen seconds.

Conor McGregor is the undisputed UFC featherweight champion of the world. It appears that his destiny has been fulfilled. The naysayers have been silenced. He has delivered on a dream that even a few years before would have appeared outlandish to most people.

A LIFE LESS ORDINARY

Centuries before the world would hear of Conor McGregor, a version of the family name was already synonymous with another legendary outlaw warrior out to make a name for himself by any means necessary. Mention the name to any proud Scotsman with even the vaguest notion of his country's history, and they'll immediately make the connection to a near mythical, but very real figure in that nation's history.

Born in 1671, Rob Roy MacGregor came to be known as the Scottish Robin Hood. One of the oldest Scottish clans, by the time Rob was born, the MacGregors made their living by cattle rustling or levying a 'black meal' or 'black rent' on their neighbors' cattle. A freebooting brigand who had frequent run-ins with the nobility, 'Red Rob' (a name he used on account of his red hair and beard) was immortalised in fiction by both Sir Walter Scott and the English poet William Wordsworth.

Conor McGregor wasn't born into a family of outlaw brigands. But he did arrive into the world, at least according to what the midwife told his mother, Margaret, with his fists clenched and ready for a fight.

Conor's father Tony, a handsome and affable man, grew up in Liverpool, the son of an Irish father and English mother. After a family split, he was sent to live with relatives in Dublin. It was here he met his future wife Margaret, an equally affable and vivacious woman. They were both only twenty-one-years-old when they married. Their daughter Erin was born a year later.

The young family settled in Crumlin, a tightly-knit, working class Dublin neighborhood. Conor's early life was characterized by its normality. While he was usually the leader of whatever group of kids he was among, he was by all accounts, quite a quiet child. In some of his interviews, especially when he talks about his teen years and wanting only to be left alone, you can glimpse the reserved child who was probably more sensitive than all but those closest to him may have given him credit for.

A keen football fan, like many kids growing up in Ireland his team was an English one, Manchester United. He played football for a local team, but his sporting interests were to switch when he was given the opportunity to box at the local Crumlin Boxing Club.

As an area, the richness and vitality of working class Crumlin is illustrated by the diverse nature of the people who either lived in or came to be associated with the area, from actor Gabriel Byrne, to writer and poet Brendan Behan, the Irish poet and painter (played by Daniel Day Lewis in the movie *My Left Foot*), Christy Brown, and of course, one of Dublin's most fondly remembered sons, Phil Lynott, the charismatic front man of rock band, *Thin Lizzy*. And that is by no means a comprehensive list.

As with many successful people, something had to shift in Conor McGregor's life to give him the initial impetus to chase his dream. It's not unheard of, but certainly rare, that people who never face any great upset or challenge in their formative years go on to achieve greatness in the way that McGregor has. In real life as in fiction, adversity is not just the catalyst, but also often the fuel, that propels people forward. A state of contentment leads only to stasis. Something has to happen to disturb a person's balance and propel them forward to their eventual goal.

In Conor McGregor's case that was a family move, when he was fifteen, from Crumlin to Lucan, a more affluent area on the very outskirts of Dublin. While moving a fifteen minute drive from where you've been living may not seem that much of a rupture to many people, at fifteen years of age, when you have already established your group of friends – friends you know and trust through the shared bond of growing up together – it's a wrench. And, as any parent of a teenager will know, at fifteen, upsets and ruptures in the fabric of normal life can take on a heightened significance.

Certainly that was the case for a young Conor McGregor. As he himself has said: "I certainly did not handle it well. I eventually did. But at the time, I had a lot resentment towards my family. I actually was really upset for a long time."

But, as with so many things in life that seem only negative at the time, there was an upside. Good came out of bad, and the angry young man used his new isolation to good effect. Cut off from his old friends, and with more time to himself, he had time to think and reflect on what he wanted from life. On who he wanted to be. And what he wanted to do.

While he may have resented his parent's decision to move, it brought with it new opportunities. Not only did he begin to broaden the scope of his interest in fighting beyond boxing, to include kick boxing and other martial arts, he forged a new friendship. It would prove to be a pivotal relationship at a critical time in his development. Conor McGregor found in Tom Egan someone of the same age who shared his passion and enthusiasm, but who also critically helped broaden his horizons in terms of MMA.

In a rare, and recently released video that was shot by Dean Kelly Photography in 2008, McGregor describes how he and Egan (who would go on to become the first Irish fighter in the UFC) met. In McGregor's own words: "I was in 5th year in school, and I moved schools, up to a school in Lucan, and Tom was one of the first friends I had. He introduced me to semi-contact kick boxing. . . I drifted back to boxing and he drifted to BJJ (Brazilian Jiu Jitsu). And every day in school that's all we'd talk about, the UFC, and Jesus, imagine how would we could get there."

It might have been the kind of starry-eyed conversation between schoolboys around the world, but in the end both of them got there. There were still a couple of pieces to be found to complete this early puzzle, and again it was Tom Egan who helped his friend locate them.

As McGregor related in the same 2008

interview with Dean Kelly: "Every weekend I'd go up to his (place) in Kildare and we'd train in a shed, and we'd literally take lumps out of each other. I'd teach him boxing and he'd teach me BJJ, and then after a few months of that he found a legit place, Straight Blast Gym, where you can go, you can compete with Irish fighters, and you can get legitimate fights in the cage. So we thought this is for us. I went up to his one Friday night, we did a good session. Saturday morning then John Kavanagh's Straight Blast Gym class started at Harold's Cross. We drove all the way down from Kildare into Harold's Cross, loved what we seen, the set up was great, the fighters were great, we felt at home."

Both McGregor and Egan had found their home. John Kavanagh would go on to become the pivotal figure in both young men's life, fulfilling the role that a trainer like the legendary boxing coach Cus D'Amato would play in the development of fighters such as Jose Torres and Mike Tyson.

But before the young Irishman could truly focus with his friend and coach on his plans for fame, fortune and world domination, he would have to negotiate perhaps the most formidable obstacle of his entire life: his Mum and Dad, and there desire to see him in a secure, paying job at a time when the Irish economy had just cratered after the collapse of its banking sector that had left the country on the edge of economic oblivion.

Conor's mother Margaret had found him a plumbing apprenticeship. In Ireland's tiger economy years, skilled tradesman such as plumbers were in high demand and consequently made good money. For a normal kid who had left school but didn't want to go to college it was an excellent opportunity. The economy would pick up, construction levels would rise, and Tony and Margaret's son would have a solid career ahead of him.

But as we now know, Conor wasn't a normal kid. He was ambitious and focussed.

He had more than dreams. He had a plan.

That plan did not include slogging his guts out on a building site for ten hours a day. It wasn't that he was scared of hard work. Far from it. But the hard work he embraced took place at John Kavanagh's Straight Blast Gym.

As quoted on US sports website, *The Bleacher Report*: "I did not see anyone who was in any kind of healthy shape. I saw that maybe if I walked away from plumbing I could train two times a day. I could really focus on my diet."

Naturally enough, his parents, and particularly his father, Tony, were less than delighted with their son's decision to turn his back on a solid career to take what must have seemed like a million-to-one shot. There was no established career path for MMA fighters in the same way that there was for young football players or even boxers. Added to that, no Irishman had made the journey yet. McGregor and his friend Tom Egan would have to conquer uncharted territory.

The young McGregor's decision put a strain on his relationship with his father. It's an age old conflict. A son who wants to strike out on his own, carve his own path and make his own journey. A father who wants to protect his son from disappointment and not throw away his future for the sake of an unattainable dream. Thankfully, for McGregor, his coach, and millions of people around the world, Conor McGregor won that particular argument.

He quit plumbing. He devoted himself to his fighting career. Now that he had gotten his own way, he had a point to prove. On March 8th, 2008, he made his professional debut.

At his side was the nucleus of the team that would accompany him to international stardom. At the very centre of that team, then as now, was John Kavanagh.

WHEN THE TEACHER IS READY

When the student is ready, the teacher appears. Or so goes the popular saying that is mostly often incorrectly attributed to Buddha. In the case of Conor McGregor and John Kavanagh it could be argued that the saying should be inverted. Kavanagh had already dedicated his life to martial arts when McGregor and Egan joined his Saturday morning class at Straight Blast. But while he had found, and trained, many dedicated, and talented fighters, he had yet to unearth a diamond in the rough with the potential of McGregor.

Some coaches can spend a lifetime waiting for the equivalent of a Conor McGregor to walk into their life. For some coaches it will simply never happen. Kavanagh did have one advantage though. Unlike other sports, if you wanted to learn MMA in Ireland your choices were limited.

None of that is in any way to take away or detract from John Kavanagh's achievements. If anything it makes what he has achieved all the more remarkable. There are advantages to being a trailblazer, but it can also be a lonely, and at times thankless, journey. There is no immediate road map. There are fewer people to draw strength from. Especially when you are the de facto leader of a group of people who look to you to help fulfill their dreams. You may have to project an air of confidence when you are far from sure about the effectiveness of what you're doing. It is a solitary existence.

Thankfully for the fighters he trains, John

Kavanagh was a man accustomed to a greater degree of solitude than most people. As with his protege, John Kavanagh's character was forged by early adversity that led to a period of reflection.

By his own admission "a very quiet kid," who "didn't have a huge amount of friends", he was introduced to karate at the age of four when his father took him to a local club. He enjoyed the solitude and calm of martial arts, an aspect often forgotten about by a media that focuses on the brutality of unarmed combat.

The pivotal moment for Kavanagh came at the age of eighteen when he was the victim of a violent assault by a group of seven people that almost ended in his death. Having studied karate for so many years his inability to defend himself led to him questioning the point of what he'd been studying, though he acknowledges that against such overwhelming numbers no amount of training would have affected the outcome.

After reflection came a new path. As Kavanagh relates in a video interview with the website *Project 1 of 6*, "I tried a few different martial arts, and then I came across UFC 1. I just thought it was fascinating."

The UFC 1 is a reference to a video tape of MMA fights that Kavanagh bought in a Dublin video store on a Friday afternoon in 1996. It was this exposure to, and fascination with, the UFC that began Kavanagh's journey. But, again in a striking parallel to Conor McGregor's journey, John too encountered a measure of well-intentioned parental resistance.

Having taken a degree in Mechanical Engineering at University College, Dublin - a decision prompted by his mother – Kavanagh opened his first MMA gym. It was rough and ready, no bigger than a two car garage, but it was his, and he was proud of it. Showing it to his parents, his mother promptly burst into tears and his father, according to Kavanagh "was like, what are you doing with your life?"

There were tough years ahead. It's all too easy to look back now and see Kavanagh's progression as some kind of straight line. That is almost never the case for someone trying to build a business in an untried sector. It's most often a journey fraught with setbacks, failures and self-doubt.

The early days were, "Just me and fifteen or twenty other guys. We just beat the hell out of each other. It was very raw back then.. . No one knew about the sport, there was no fame, there was no career path in it."

Beyond the obvious early challenges of finding somewhere to run his school, and recruiting fighters, Kavanagh also had some personal issues to deal with. Looking back, he describes those issues with an unflinching honesty and rare degree of self-awareness. "I guess I was dealing with some stuff from when I was growing up. I used to kind of see maybe the school bully on the other side of the Octagon. And then once I had maybe worked my way through that and let that side go, I felt a weight off my shoulders."

As American self-help guru Anthony Robbins posits, "The mind follows the body, the body follows the mind." Using MMA to work through his own fears and anger has left Kavanagh as a supremely relaxed individual. He comes across as a man remarkably at ease with the world and comfortable in his own skin.

It's a quality I recognise from the high-end private security operatives and lifers in Pelican Bay Supermax that I've met as research for my fiction. To be at ease with your masculinity, sense of self and physicality often involves confronting your worst fears and insecurities. Men who have lived with violence, and used it with measured control to shape their world, are often the most relaxed, and least macho individuals you will encounter.

Having dealt with his own issues, Kavanagh set about building a group of ambitious young MMA fighters. There would be many disappointments, failures and set backs, but like all great coaches Kavanagh understood that these could, and should be seen as opportunities to learn and progress for his young group of fighters.

Kavanagh's emphasis on the process of learning MMA rather than just cashing results, would prove key. He understood that both he and his small group of fighters would fail many times before they turned things around. Both individually and collectively a long, lonely path lay ahead of them.

The only way to conquer the world of MMA was to put in the work. Day after day. Week after week. Month after month. All the time accepting that in Brazil, the United States, and the United

Kingdom, other trainers and other fighters were doing the same.

Where perhaps Kavanagh's fighters had an edge was in their trainer's emphasis on technique. While an MMA fight can look to the unschooled eye like a random and chaotic brawl, underpinning the action is a very complex array of physical movements. Not only must these movements be committed to memory, to the point where they are automatic, they must also be performed with precision.

That is where a coach's assessment and feedback comes in. Like a director with an actor, part of the role of a coach is to provide an objective view and suggest adjustments and refinements to techniques, that when put together with physical conditioning and strategy, will raise the overall level of performance of the fighter.

In terms of fight preparation part of John Kavanagh's success has stemmed from his ability to analyse the fighting style, strengths and weaknesses of the opponent his fighter would face. But he had one additional quality that McGregor recognized even as a teenager. Unlike other coaches and trainers, Kavanagh wasn't dogmatic when it came to how things should be done. As McGregor noted in a 2015 interview with Setanta Sports, "He (Kavanagh) had a more open mind, and he encouraged different movements, and I'd never experienced that before."

Whether it was his interest in mechanical engineering and mathematics, his college degree, or simply his own intellectual curiosity, Kavanagh did not fit the stereotype of someone who trains young people in combat sports. A quote from Muhammad Ali, framed and hung on the wall of his gym summarized an attitude that would emphasis dedication, preparation and sacrifice as the cornerstones of what they would build together.

"The fight is won or lost far away from witnesses, behind the lines, in the gym, and out there on the road, long before I dance under those lights." Muhammad Ali

It was this emphasis on preparation and hard work that underpinned Kavanagh's success. But he also recognized that hard work alone would not be enough. You also needed a vision of what you wanted to achieve, and where you wanted to get to. Although Ireland's influence on the world, particularly in terms of culture and arts, is wildly disproportionate to its size and population, it is worth bearing in mind that it is a small nation on the very edge of Europe. It can be, at times, parochial and inward-looking, but it has also produced individuals with courage, vision and the grit to battle against the odds.

All that said, when John Kavanagh was starting out he faced two major problems. The first was geographical location and the isolation that brought with it. MMA was barely a blip on the radar in Ireland, or Europe for that matter. Never mind any kind of broader infrastructure, there wasn't even the kind of public interest there to financially sustain the sport. Secondly the UFC, the sports premier organization was a very long way from the slick, efficient promotional juggernaut that it is today.

A lot had to happen, on both sides of Atlantic, to make Conor McGregor's ascent possible. Quite simply, when Kavanagh was starting out, and McGregor started training, the climb ahead of them was going to be arduous but the financial and cultural peak they could reach was more of a small hill than a mountain.

Much wider political, social and economic forces would have to be overcome by those who wanted to take MMA into the mainstream before it would be ready for a figure like McGregor. While the individuals behind the UFC take some flak for the amount of control they exert over MMA, it's worth recognizing the incredible obstacles they have faced in creating what is claimed to be the world's fastest growing sport.

FIRST BLOOD

Before the modern era of what became to be know as mixed martial arts, there was the ancient Greek combat sport of pankration. Pankration was a mixture of boxing and wrestling that was one of the first Olympic sports.

In the modern era, the roots of MMA lie in Brazil where rival martial arts gyms would stage *Vale Tudo ('anything goes')* contests that pitted their signature fighting styles against each other.

Central to combat sports in Brazil was the Gracie family. The Gracie name is still rightly venerated by anyone with even the most superficial knowledge of MMA, and more specifically jiu jitsu, a devastatingly effective form of grappling that became an intrinsic part of the wider sport. Simply put, without the Gracie family, and in particular Rorion Gracie, the multi-billion dollar Ultimate Fighting Championship would not exist.

Moving to the United States in the 1970s, Rorion Gracie set about popularising his family's Brazilian variant of jiu jitsu. As his BJJ school flourished, he began to make contacts with people such as ad man Art Davie and Hollywood maverick, John Milius. To get the word out about the superiority of the Gracie fighting style, and as a way of making money, Gracie and Davie began selling video tapes of contests staged by Gracie via mail order.

But mail order was a limited distribution channel that catered to a niche of people who sought out the video tapes. Davie knew that if you wanted to reach a wider audience you had to widen the channel, and the way to do that was via television. What they had was way too niche for the major American broadcast networks, so they went to cable outfit HBO. HBO turned them down. After all, HBO had boxing, a sport that at the time had the kind of excitement around it that MMA has now.

Davie and Gracie refused to give up. Finally they partnered with Semaphore Entertainment Group. SEG, with a track record in rock concerts, could offer the crucial distribution element.

John Milius, a student and friend of Rorion Gracie, offered his name to the venture. Milius, a Hollywood screenwriter and director (*Apocalypse Now, Red Dawn, Conan the Barbarian*), is a larger than life figure capable of making McGregor, or anyone else for that matter, look positively shy and retiring.

Milius is also a man given to extravagant flights of fancy. He famously suggested *Apocalypse Now* be shot on location in Vietnam while the war was still going on ("We would have been just in time for the Tet offensive!"). His suggestion prompted George Lucas (the director was originally attached) to wryly observe that he (Lucas) was going to be one who had to go over there and shoot it.

Milius' original idea for the staging of the first UFC contest was a wooden pit. After various ideas were kicked around, ranging from the impractical (plexiglass) to the positively bonkers (a moat filled with alligators surrounding the fighting space), everyone involved settled on the idea of the fights taking place in an octagonal cage.

The Octagon is the primary feature that remains almost completely unaltered, from the first UFC event, UFC 1, a videotape of which sparked John Kavanagh's interest in MMA. The Octagon offered a number of practical advantages to the new sport. Viewers tuning in knew immediately that it wasn't a boxing match. The enclosed nature prevented fighters falling out and sustaining further injury. And crucially it was TV production friendly allowing for a greater range of angles.

But fights taking place in an enclosed metal cage also provided a ready-made gift to MMA's detractors. Detractors who weren't about to let something as basic as rational examination or even any attempt to understand the nature of martial arts get in the way of their moral outrage. Almost from day one, the UFC had an image problem.

It's fair to say that some of the early UFC contests bordered on the surreal. A four hundred pound Samoan Sumo wrestler (Telia Tuli) having his teeth literally kicked out of his head by a Dutch karate black belt half his size isn't something you see every day. Not even on cable TV. Neither for that matter was witnessing a hulking boxer, Art Jimmerson, being taken to the ground and choked out by BJJ master, Royce Gracie. Of course, testing one form of unarmed combat against another form was the point. But that didn't lessen the freak show aura. Exciting. Compelling. Fascinating. It had all those qualities. But the early events also gave its later detractors a lot of ammunition.

Needless to say the early, unstructured, and arguably naive incarnation of the UFC soon ran into a public image problem. The problem soon became a storm, whipped up by the media, and picked up by commentators and eventually by legislators. It's a rare politician who hasn't met a public outcry they haven't got on board with, and US Senator John McCain proved no exception. Infamously dubbing MMA "human cockfighting", McCain and other legislators, mostly at the State level, set about making life difficult for the UFC and the wider MMA community.

While early UFC shows proved wildly popular, attracting incredible pay-per-view numbers for such a young sport, a wider moral panic had set in. Several fighters were threatened with being fired from their coaching jobs if they participated. Judges began to get involved, issuing edicts that re-wrote the rules where they couldn't actually stop an event.

Senator John McCain, who would go on to lose his own contest for President to Barack Obama, was head of the Commerce Commission. He was vehemently opposed to MMA in general, and the UFC in particular. There were also regulatory opponents and enemies within the cable television industry. Getting events on TV proved increasingly difficult. The New York Times got involved, as did New York's Mayor Rudy Giuliani. Having voted to legalize the sport, New York legislators promptly did a 180 degree turn and banned it. A ban only finally lifted in March of this year.

The UFC in its early incarnation continued for a time, but with so many powerful forces ranged against it, the writing was on the wall. Even though rules were changed, and many early problems ironed out, it was time for a fresh start. In 2001 the UFC promotion was sold by Semaphore Entertainment Group to Zuffa, a company set up by two Las Vegas casino owners, brothers Frank and Lorenzo Fertitta.

Bringing in Dana White to run the business, the Fertittas set about reforming (at least in PR terms), and rebuilding the UFC as the sport's premier promotional vehicle. They had the money, connections, and in White, a likable, not to mention credible frontman to go out and build a supremely slick sporting and media organization that is, in business terms, vertically integrated and enjoying the kind of growth that many investors would kill for.

But no matter how savvy the business people, and how slick the operation, they still rely on finding and promoting fighters who garner attention. And in Conor McGregor they were to collide with a personality who had three key qualities. He could fight and fight well. He knew how to promote. And, he understood the parameters of the business that both he, and the UFC, were operating within.

In other words, they had a showman who truly knew how to play the game, both inside and outside the Octagon.

THE CLIMB

While the UFC project was busy undergoing renovations, Conor McGregor was back home in Dublin having traded an apprenticeship in plumbing for one in fighting. It may have been many things, but glamorous it was not. He was no longer halfway up a mountain, labouring on a building site in the freezing cold, but the work ahead of him was equally as demanding.

McGregor started, as does every eventual UFC contender (and the thousands who never make it to that level), by fighting in small, local MMA contests that are literally and figuratively thousands of miles away from the glittering lights of Las Vegas. His professional debut came on March 8th, 2008 in a small Dublin promotion dubbed Cage of Truth 2 with a second round win over another Irish MMA fighter, Gary Morris. He was 19 years of age.

Less than three months later he was back in the Octagon and this time won in the first round. It was a solid start and he was keen to maintain momentum.

His third fight was his first loss. He was submitted by Artemij Sitenkov, a Lithuanian fighter. A submission in a MMA contest comes when one fighter 'taps out', literally tapping the canvas or other fighter to indicate that they give up. It is, as the name suggests, a type of loss that carries more psychological baggage for a fighter than losing a decision or the referee stopping the contest.

McGregor's ability to deal not only with losing, but with being submitted in a professional contest was pivotal. Implicit in sport is losing. The greatest teams and individuals will lose. The only way to avoid a loss is simple. You can choose not to compete.

McGregor's reaction was a demonstration of his character. On December 12th of the same year he was back in business, finishing young Irish fighter, Stephen Bailey in just one minute and twenty-two seconds. It was a brutally efficient reaction to having lost. A video of the fight shows McGregor at the end of the contest rushing over to the camera, looking straight down the lens and declaring, "I'm the fucking future!'"

Watching these early contests, some of which are available on video sharing sites such as Vimeo and Youtube, it's hard to imagine what was to come. Ireland is a small country, and MMA was a tiny, almost niche sport. It had die-hard devotees but the audience at these events would have been composed primarily of other fighters and coaches along with friends and family members.

The trademark McGregor intensity and self belief was already there, but he was still only twenty, a time in most young men's lives where there are plenty of distractions and other activities competing for their interest. After bouncing back from defeat with a decisive victory, McGregor took a break.

In an interview with Irish sports broadcaster

Setanta, he discussed what led up to his walking away, albeit temporarily, from a promising start. According to McGregor, "You're a young kid, you're just floating in and out. I was going out with my friends. You're not a million percent focussed when you're a kid. You're off doing other stuff."

It was John Kavanagh who pulled him back in, following a phone call to the coach from McGregor's mother. Of that intervention, McGregor had this to say in the same interview, "She recognised that any time I was in the gym, I was happy."

Between his family and John Kavanagh, McGregor eventually decided to pick up where he had left off. From his comeback fight in October of 2010, McGregor established a pattern of training hard, fighting frequently, learning from every contest, and winning. Barring a solitary defeat to Joseph Duffy a month after his comeback, McGregor was about to begin a winning streak that was going to catapult him to the global fame and riches that he had always envisioned.

But being a ruthless, efficient fighter was only part of the overall McGregor package. The other part was the creation of a public persona that would divide opinion, captivate the world's media, and in the process sell tens of thousands of tickets, millions of pay-per-view buys and drive record revenue to the UFC.

In marketing terms, the UFC may have been able to provide the steak, but McGregor brought the sizzle.

NOTORIOUS

Most if not all boxers and MMA fighters adopt, or are given, a nickname. McGregor dubbed himself 'The Notorious'. While it's still used, it is a testament to what he has achieved that nowadays it seems almost superfluous. His own name carries more than enough brand recognition in and of itself. But in the early part of his career adopting a moniker allowed him to begin the process of creating a public persona that he could use to leverage his growing athletic abilities.

The persona he created drew on traits that were already present. McGregor is undeniably bright, engaging and quick-witted. But in early interviews, and when he talks about growing up, there are also glimpses of someone who is, in opposition to what the world thinks of him, an introvert and a thinker. Indeed, in several interviews, he says that what drew him to boxing and then martial arts was how he brooded after he got into fights as a teenager. In an interview with Esquire magazine he admitted straight out that, "The reason I got into the game was so that people would leave me the fuck alone", going on to to add, "It's backfired on me."

It's likely for this very reason that McGregor sticks to the public persona he has developed over a number of years. He surely realised some time ago that dealing with the media, and in particular with journalists, is a double-edge sword. You need them in order to promote yourself and make a living, but they are more than happy to tear people down when the mood strikes them or it suits their agenda.

Outside the world of sports, entertainment and the media, most people wouldn't realise that McGregor's promotional activities, up to and including interviews, are part of his contractual obligation. Throw in freelance paparazzi, and videographers, along with websites like TMZ and when you reach McGregor's level of fame you have a level of scrutiny that most celebrities struggle to deal with.

Starting out though, McGregor knew that fighting ability alone would not be enough to take him where he wanted to go. He had to be a showman, and a salesman if he was to achieve his full potential as a fighter.

The first building block was a seemingly unshakeable belief in his own abilities. Allied to that belief was a level of ambition that at the time must have seemed ludicrous to many. Irish fighters didn't make it to the UFC, never mind win championship belts. It was a sport all but dominated by Brazilians and Americans.

Again, the very early interviews that can be found show McGregor as both confident and supremely ambitious. In 2008 he said that, "My dream is to be world champion in the UFC, have more money than I know what do with, and have a great life for my kids, my grandkids, everyone in my family, everyone that's come up with me. That's my dream."

Lots of young men, and women, dream of fame and fortune. What set McGregor apart was his dedication. He dedicated himself to his newfound vocation. He put in the long hard hours. He made sacrifices. His discipline extended to his diet, which for a serious MMA fighter has to be strict.

It's also revealing that even this early on he talked about achievement in terms of what it would allow him to do for his family and friends. It demonstrated a maturity and level of emotional intelligence that would stand him in good stead later on. By having a core group of people around him whom he could trust, he could focus on his career without having to worry about competing agendas.

Along with his coach, family, and the fighters from Straight Blast Gym, he had a long-term girlfriend, Dee Devlin. Being in a settled relationship gave him stability and allowed him to concentrate on his career. She was far more than a pretty girl to have on his arm. She not only believed in him, she believed in that he could and would achieve his goals. Providing crucial support when he needed it most, Dee would become integral to his success.

In early interviews you can see McGregor trying on his new public persona for size, and adjusting accordingly. In a scene from an early documentary about his journey he is in a hotel room with John Kavanagh. He flicks through a book, *The Key to Living the Law of Attraction*, reading a series of aphorisms out loud. He then observes, "When I read quotes and shit, I take from them, and just put my own thing to it. Say it in my own way."

In later press conferences and interviews, McGregor will deploy just this tactic to great effect. Not only does it lend him an extra dimension that most of the other UFC fighters lack, his deployment of highly quotable aphorisms ("Humble in victory, humble in defeat") begin to lead reporters toward the inevitable comparisons with Ali.

Beyond the PR value, McGregor's interest in books like the one above also demonstrates his innate curiosity about not only movement and fighting techniques, but ideas. Away from the cage, or the gym, many fighters can appear dull and unengaged. McGregor however is the opposite. He is fully engaged, both physically and mentally, always looking to improve, constantly seeking new insights that will allow him to recalibrate his approach. And not just his approach inside the Octagon, but outside it as well. Early on in his career, McGregor realised that he can begin to weaken his opponents in the weeks leading up to a fight.

It's easy to see McGregor's press conference posturing and trash talk as an indication of an over-inflated ego. It's also incredibly naive. It took many MMA fans, and especially supporters of his opponents, a while to realise that when McGregor is verbally provocative and insulting, he does it for a reason.

McGregor's trash talk serves two purposes, both of which benefit him enormously. It makes him the focus of attention by providing a great angle for the media. But he also uses it to forensically pull apart, and psychologically weaken his opponents before he fights them. In this respect the parallels with Muhammad Ali hold up.

Ali famously first located, then probed, and ultimately exploited his opponents' psychological weaknesses. In the case of his fight with Sonny Liston, Ali went so far as driving a bus onto the front lawn of Liston's home at three clock in the morning, and shouting "Come on out of there. I'm gonna whip you now." Ali subsequently pretended to be crazy at the weigh-in for the fight because, "Liston's not afraid of me, but he's afraid of a nut." In the fight that followed, Liston spat out his mouth guard and refused to come out of his corner for the seventh round. Ali was declared the winner.

Although McGregor hasn't gone as far as driving onto an opponent's front lawn in the middle of the night, not yet anyway, he has employed similar tactics to disrupt, enrage, and undermine opponents. His taunting of Jose Aldo was a masterclass in psychological warfare that Ali himself would have been proud of. And, like Ali, McGregor uses his sense of humour and quick wits to land verbal shots. Up close and personal most MMA fighters, especially world champions, tend to command respect. They are not used to be laughed at or openly mocked. McGregor does both.

As his career has matured, McGregor has begun to add other elements to his public persona.

Known for his tailor made suits, since he debuted in the UFC his body has become the canvas for an increasing number of elaborate tattoos. While he claims there's no special meaning behind the ink on his body, they, along with his dress sense, have augmented Brand McGregor. In or out of the ring, he is now almost instantly recognisable. His changing image may also be testament to the fact that he is constantly evolving.

But image and trash talk are not what have made McGregor a global star. His rise through the ranks of the UFC came about because of a stunning run of victories. As has been so often said, he could talk the talk, but he also walked the walk.

THE CALL

As the UFC's point man, Dana White is always looking for fresh blood in the form of new fighters he can bring into the UFC. Every place he visits has its own local hero or rising star. Not all of them are ready to make the jump. Or when they do, they are unable to cope with the pressure that fighting in the UFC brings and deliver the goods. It's one thing to claim to be ready to compete at the highest level, it's quite another to actually do it. By the time McGregor met Dana White he was more than just ready, he was more than just hungry, he was ravenous.

As White relates it, "I was in Ireland and everyone was coming up to me, and talking about Conor McGregor. We ended up flying him out here, and I had dinner with him. And when I left that dinner, I called my partner Lorenzo and I said, 'I don't know if this guy can fight or not, but if he can even throw a punch this kid is gonna be a huge superstar."

While it makes for a good story, Dana White would already have been well aware of McGregor's abilities as a fighter. McGregor had a growing and formidable reputation as someone who fought often, and won.

In actuality, the story White tells should have been inverted. The UFC knew they had a great prospect in McGregor, his record in Ireland told them that, but what they didn't know they were also going to get was the personality. That was what White realised when he finally sat down with McGregor. Here was someone that White instantly knew could be very special indeed. Just how special? It's fair to say that no-one, apart from McGregor himself and perhaps his coach John Kavanagh, had any idea just how much of a box office draw the new kid on the block would prove to be.

McGregor's first UFC fight took place in Stockholm, Sweden on the 6th of April, 2013. He was matched against Marcus Brimage, an American fighter known as the 'Bama Beast. 'Bama being short for Brimage's home state of Alabama.

Brimage, who had been inspired to learn martial arts by watching Japanese anime cartoon Dragon Ball Z, wore a futuristic looking mask inspired by the cartoon series to the weigh-in. This prompted the typically quick-witted McGregor to tell Brimage, "You're 28-years-old, you shouldn't be wearing a superhero mask." Suitably needled, the two fighters almost came close to blows. McGregor, as would so often be the case, had landed the first shot using only his mouth.

Having quickly gotten under Brimage's skin, McGregor, with no sponsor, entered the arena with no shirt and draped in the Irish flag. Stepping into the Octagon, he made short work of Brimage. To borrow a Scottish term, McGregor molligated Brimage. After a series of powerful upper cuts, Brimage went down. McGregor pursued him onto the floor, and the referee stopped the fight. It had lasted just 67 seconds.

McGregor had begun his UFC career with a decisive victory that earned him a $60,000 bonus for the knockout of the night. At the post-fight press conference, McGregor gave what was to become a trademark performance that immediately won over the assembled journalists and media.

Asked about where this fight figured in his career so far McGregor's candid answer drew laughter from the audience. Noting that this was his biggest and best result so far, he went on to say that up until now he had been claiming social welfare and now he'd just won sixty thousand dollars. His obvious delight in making that much money in a single night put everyone in the room, including his fellow fighters, firmly on his side. McGregor was on his way, and his main concern now was to maintain his momentum.

His second fight brought him to Boston. With its huge Irish-American population, it may as well have been a hometown fight for McGregor. Even though his fight was not the main event, it seemed like no one had told the crowd. Again making his entrance draped in the Irish flag, he was greeted by a deafening roar. As a nod to his newfound star status, the UFC also dimmed the lights inside the arena, giving him what is known in the trade as a blackout.

His opponent was 21-year-old Max Holloway, at the time the UFC's second youngest fighter. Taller than McGregor, but with a shorter reach, he was a serious opponent who offered a stouter challenge than Brimage had.

A brave fighter, Holloway soaked up the punishment meted out by McGregor in the first round. In the second round, McGregor felt his knee pop out and had to adjust his approach. He went on to win by decision. Despite being injured he had managed to secure another win, having never looked like being beaten at any point.

But the injury, which turned out to be a torn ACL (a serious injury for anyone, never mind an MMA fighter), would slow him up. It would be almost a year before he fought again. If Boston had felt like a hometown fight, his next fight would take place in his actual hometown of Dublin. The UFC, whose stated ambition has been to make MMA the world's most popular sport, saw a way of capitalising on McGregor's increasing profile in Ireland and took it.

The 19th of July, 2014, saw McGregor headline a UFC event in Dublin. It was a quite remarkable achievement. The event sold out in record time. The UFC's Dana White, knowing how incredible the Irish crowd would be, went out and bought equipment that would record the volume level inside the O2 Arena.

McGregor was up against a tough Brazilian fighter, Diego Brandao, after his original opponent, Cole Miller, had dropped out. Fighters slated to fight McGregor dropping out would become a feature of McGregor's career. With Brandao in place the build up to the fight was frenetic but broadly uneventful until the weigh-in when the two men almost came to blows.

The event featured a number of Irish fighters, but McGregor was the undoubted star of the show. Brandao, whose career was on the wane, offered a flinty performance, but proved no match for McGregor who stopped him near the end of the first round.

Dana White's decibel meter recorded a reading of 111 decibels from the Irish crowd as McGregor finished Brandao off. A rock concert, White noted the next day, is only 110 decibels.

While his Irish fans only adored McGregor all the more, even at this stage he was proving to be a character who divided opinion. He was either loved or hated. The hate was almost exclusively generated by his pre and post fight pronouncements. There was also a longstanding belief, not without some truth, that as an organisation the UFC liked to play favourites.

In many ways the accusation that McGregor was being given special treatment was true. But McGregor's detractors didn't stop to ask why. The reality was, and is, that McGregor was box office dynamite. If some people hated what they saw as his rampant ego and lack of respect for others, well, that only drove the interest in him all the more. McGregor had never adjusted his approach to satisfy his critics. With his star in the ascendancy, he sure as hell wasn't about to start now. If people didn't like him then that was there problem.

In terms of special treatment, or being

favoured by the UFC top brass, there was another factor at play. McGregor was savvy enough to play the game on the UFC's terms. He did everything that was asked of him and more. He was a workhorse, not just in terms of his training and fight preparation, but also when it came to honouring his media commitments and helping to build not just his own brand, but the UFC brand as a whole.

Many fighters when they began to gain success were capable of acting like prima donnas or as Dana White has phrased it, of 'getting goofy.' McGregor wasn't about to blow all his hard work now. He was proving to be the perfect mixture of maverick entertainer and hardheaded pragmatist. His reward for the success of the Dublin event was the chance to take on another contender for world champion, Dustin Poirier.

Ahead of McGregor was a run of fights that would lead him towards the championship belt. But as with so much in his life there would be a few surprises along the way.

THE SUMMIT

Sport, especially at the elite level, is political. Even more so when you throw billions of dollars into the mix. The people who own and operate the UFC can quite literally make or break a fighter's career. While no one forces a fighter into the Octagon, the UFC selects his or her opponents, where they will appear on the card, and decides the date, and location of the contest, as well as negotiating with the fighter and their representatives the payment they will receive.

This level of control has been key to the rapid growth in the popularity of MMA. Anyone who doubts this need only look at the fragmented, and increasingly ramshackle world of professional boxing, MMA's closest competitor. In a very short space of time the current owners and operators of the UFC have built a slick, efficient, and dynamic promotional organisation on top of the already solid foundation they inherited from the UFC's originators.

At the same time, without the fighters, MMA as a sport and the UFC as a spectacle, doesn't exist. The UFC needs fighters, and because of the promotional and distribution systems they have built, fighters need the UFC. The third and crucial element, and in many ways the pre-eminent one, are the fans. Both casual and die-hard, they are the people who, by purchasing tickets and pay-per-view subscriptions, ensure that everyone gets paid and the events can take place.

Unlike other sports there is no pre-scheduled list of who will compete against each other. Instead what you have are fighters being matched against each other. Because of the nature of the training (something the UFC is keen to address), injuries before a fight are commonplace. Competitors drop out. Replacements are found. Fans and commentators lobby hard online via message boards, podcasts and social media for their favourites to given certain matches. It's not unusual for Dana White and the UFC to take the temperature among the fans before matching one fighter against another. It's simply good business to give fans the fights that they are clamoring for.

Ultimately though, the UFC are the final arbiters of who fights and when. Many fans see this as leading to certain fighters being given preferential treatment, and in the case of someone like McGregor, being fast-tracked up the ranks. Fighters who don't get the match ups they want are often understandably bitter and resentful.

There is however a problem with the conspiracy theories that circulate online. The UFC exists to promote the sport, but also to make money and generate a profit. It stands to reason therefore that it will focus on fighters who capture the broadest audience, and in doing so, generate the most money. It's also the case that for a fighter to reach the highest levels they have to win.

McGregor's rapid ascent came down to three main factors that the UFC were never going to ignore. First, McGregor was a winner. Second, he had the character and persona to not only draw strong reactions from existing fans, but to draw in people who had never taken much of an interest in MMA. In other words, he could shift the needle and grow the market rather than just take share. Third, as previously stated, he played the promotional game with a natural flair.

His fight with Dustin Poirier would take him to the capital of the UFC, Las Vegas, Nevada, and a meeting with a fighter that many fans believed would test McGregor to the limits. In the featherweight division, Poirier had the most wins and most finishes of any fighter.

Poirier's record bred confidence. Ahead of the fight, Poirier claimed that, "This is gonna be good for him (McGregor). He needs an ass whooping like he's about to get. It's gonna make him a better person in the long run."

Unfortunately for Poirier who himself had his gaze firmly set on the world championship belt, the young Irishman had other ideas. This was a Conor McGregor who already seemed to be light years away from the young man who had appeared at the press conference in Sweden where he talked about having to inform the social welfare office in Dublin that he was signing off the dole. His self belief, a quality that had always been there, was much more on show. Confidence had begun to manifest itself, at least according to his critics, as arrogance.

The build up to the fight revealed a genuine animosity toward McGregor by Poirier. Poirier's dislike of McGregor and what he saw as his arrogance should have been a warning sign.

McGregor's psychological warfare was already beginning to pay off. McGregor and his camp quite correctly calculated that an opponent who is emotionally engaged is far more likely to make a mistake.

It's a paradox of MMA, a sport that is premised on the deployment of violence, that anger is a dangerous emotion to indulge. McGregor's reaction when shown footage of how personally Poirier was taking the whole thing was revealing. He burst out laughing.

The weigh-in, where both fighters take to the scales before facing off, was a boisterous affair. It was becoming a trademark of McGregor that he could draw more of his fans (most of whom had travelled the thousands of miles from Ireland) to a simple weigh-in than many fighters could attract to an actual fight.

Some fans came to see him win. Others were there to see him put in his place. Either way, the result was the same. Record ticket sales and pay-per-view buys.

With the posturing and trash talk out of the way, it was time for the question of who was the better fighter to be settled. When it came down to it, it was not a question that took too long to be answered.

McGregor had already predicted that he would win in the first round. His habit of predicting not just the time but the manner in which he would win had earned him the sobriquet Mystic Mac. No doubt it also served an additional psychological purpose by placing an additional question mark in the mind of his opponent.

In the initial exchanges, Dustin Poirier held his own. McGregor threatened, Poirier countered, and it looked like it may be a contest. Then just over ninety seconds into the fight after McGregor was starting to dominate, he caught Poirier with a glancing blow to the back of the head. Poirier went down, McGregor followed him, and unleashed a series of ferocious blows before the referee stepped in to stop the fight.

Mystic Mac's prophecy had come true. McGregor was now beyond a shadow of a doubt the prime contender to fight the reigning champion of the division, Jose Aldo.

However Aldo would have to wait, at least for the time being.

CHASING ALDO

2015 was slated to be Conor McGregor's year, and so it proved. In January he was back in the cage. But rather than fighting Jose Aldo for the world championship belt, he faced German UFC veteran Dennis Siver. So would began a frustrating pursuit of the reigning champ by McGregor as he tried to get Aldo inside the Octagon to fight.

McGregor was the heavy favourite to beat Siver. There was excitement around the contest but it was mostly generated by McGregor who seemed to be relishing his ability to divide opinion. As he said in an interview before the Siver fight, "Hate is a beautiful thing to me. I love it. The whole roster can hate me. The whole of America can hate me. I only need one American to love me, and that is Mr. Benjamin Franklin."

In fact, the Siver fight was to take place in Boston where McGregor was guaranteed a warm welcome from his growing traveling fan base and the city's massive Irish-American population. Before the fight two things came across very clearly. McGregor was having the time of his life, and Siver was getting riled up by what McGregor was saying. Once again McGregor's opponent had fallen into the trap of personalising the contest in their own mind. Siver had taken the bait and become emotionally invested in beating McGregor. Although Siver edging out McGregor, even with a clear head, was unlikely, his loss of focus didn't help matters.

On the evening of the fight, McGregor's bout was the main event. He was accorded another blackout as the stadium lights were dimmed for his entrance. In what was another record breaking UFC gate for the Boston venue, he was greeted with the usual roar and the sight of dozens of Irish flags.

Inside the cage, the fight began and it didn't take very long for McGregor to demonstrate his dominance. He appeared to be toying with Siver. By the end of the first round, Siver was in trouble, but he made it to the bell.

The second round was more of the same. McGregor's unorthodox style allied to his sheer power and technical ability meant Siver was quickly in trouble again. What appeared to be no more than a glancing blow to the back of Siver's head signaled the beginning of the end. His face already bloodied from McGregor's punches, he went down.

McGregor followed him to the canvas, straddled him and unleashed a precise volley of fresh shots to Siver's head. The referee Herb Dean had seen enough.

So far, so predictable. But there was more excitement to come.

McGregor had spotted Jose Aldo sitting in the front row. Climbing out of the Octagon, McGregor went to confront him. Security stepped in to ensure McGregor didn't get too close as the Brazilian smiled.

By confronting Aldo, McGregor had provided a fresh talking point. It would be the start of a brutal, unrelenting war of words directed against the reigning Brazilian champion by the young Irishman. Barely five seconds after he had dispatched Siver, McGregor had already begun his campaign of psychological warfare against his next opponent. He had also effectively provided the UFC with millions of dollars in free advertising as the moment went viral.

There was no question that McGregor had earned the right to fight for the championship belt. His case was now irrefutable. Not just because of his win record, and the ease with which he had dispatched his opponents. But also because he was proving to be a record draw. He was the fighter that fans old and new wanted to see above any other. The raw data proved that.

DUCK AND WEAVE

At the start of 2015 Jose Aldo was regarded as the best pound for pound fighter in MMA. There was a certain mystique around him. It was a mystique that had been well earned. It had been a long time since he'd been beaten. He'd successfully defended his title on numerous occasions.

Beyond his record, Aldo's story was a remarkable one. Born in the Amazon region of Brazil, his upbringing was one of grinding poverty. Like McGregor he dreamed of competing in the UFC, but his path there was arguably much tougher. Early on in his career his coaches would give him food because he didn't have enough money to eat.

When placed in the context of what he had overcome to get where he had, Jose Aldo was never going to react well to what he saw as McGregor's lack of respect. But again what many MMA fans, especially the die-hards, saw as a lack of class in McGregor's taunting of Aldo, McGregor saw as a method of psychological warfare that would unsettle his opponent.

From the moment he climbed out of the cage to confront Aldo in Boston, McGregor launched a sustained verbal attack on the champion. When the UFC announced that the two men would indeed meet in Las Vegas on the 11th of July, 2015, things got more heated.

A twelve day press tour with the two fighters

covered five countries in three continents. As the tour went on the insults traded between the two men became increasingly personal and ill-tempered. Just as before, McGregor seemed to be enjoying every single second of it, even at the first event in Brazil when the crowd drowned out McGregor's answers with a chant that roughly translates to "You're going to die." Such a reaction from Aldo's fans was meat and drink to McGregor.

McGregor made sure that the Dublin event to promote the fight was equally uncomfortable for Aldo. At one point McGregor reached over and swiped Aldo's belt, drawing a furious reaction from the champion.

To say that Aldo didn't appreciate McGregor's conduct is an understatement. Watching the two men face off it's clear to see that McGregor saw it as all just a game, while Aldo took the insults to heart. It's probably also fair to say that there were times where McGregor seemed to over-step the mark. Having signed a sponsorship deal with Reebok before the fight with Siver, McGregor's comment that he planned to turn Aldo's "favella into a Reebok sweatshop" was perhaps not the Irish fighter's proudest moment.

With the UFC having spent considerable money to hype the fight into the stratosphere, a matter of weeks before their match-up, Aldo withdrew, citing a rib injury that he hadn't recovered from. McGregor, who had fought injured, was understandably less than impressed. Going on record, McGregor scornfully noted that, "Doctors have cleared him to fight – it's a bruise –

but he still pulled out."

The UFC were also disappointed. Aldo who hadn't learned English (something that would have helped him considerably in what was an increasingly global sport), and spent most of his time in Brazil, was likely seen by the organisation as not being a team player.

McGregor on the other hand pulled out all the stops to promote. For fans who saw, and still see, the UFC and Dana White as playing favourites with McGregor, that was the explanation right there. McGregor got on board with marketing, press and promotion not because he enjoyed it (it's clear from many comments that it's work to him and he finds it draining), but because that was what was required of him.

There was one additional element to Aldo's late withdrawal. It may seem ridiculous for anyone to accuse a character like Aldo of being fearful, but the question mark was there none the less. It's one thing to go into a fight knowing that you'll better your opponent. It's quite another to enter the cage with the knowledge that you may be beaten. Especially when you are a reigning champion. It was an accusation that McGregor would later ensure couldn't be leveled at him when he made an audacious decision about an opponent. But that was further down the line.

The UFC now had to find a replacement for Aldo, and fast. To his credit, Chad Mendes stepped forward to fill Aldo's shoes. Mendes had the incentive that there would be a huge payday for whoever replaced Aldo.

There was no doubt anxiety about how well the event would do now that the much hyped showdown between champ and challenger was no more. But the McGregor train proved to have more than enough momentum to obviate any huge loss in interest. Champion or not, at this stage, 'The Notorious' Conor McGregor was the show.

Mendes had already fought Jose Aldo. He lost the decision after the fight went the duration. It had been an epic battle. He had followed up this points loss with a first round win over Ricardo Lamas. As such, he was seen as offering McGregor a real challenge, in particular because his strength in wrestling and fighting on the ground was seen as McGregor's weak area.

In the pre-fight press conference, McGregor baited Mendes and Mendes reacted. The pattern was becoming predictable. To his credit though, Mendes did seem a good deal cooler and less emotional than Aldo had been when confronted with McGregor's jibes. He shot back insults at McGregor, but it all seemed a little half-hearted on both their parts.

The weigh-in provided further proof of McGregor's bankability. Ten thousand fans packed into the MGM Grand Garden Arena to see the fighters stand on the scales. The overwhelmingly Irish crowd prompted UFC commentator Joe Rogan to quip that "This does not feel like Vegas. It feels like Dublin." It was proof of McGregor's much vaunted claim that the Irish weren't in town to take part, they were there to take over.

The fight itself proved to be perhaps McGregor's sternest test to date. On the night, Mendes did not appear to be intimidated by the Irishman. Indeed the scoring had him winning the first round. It looked unlikely that Mystic Mac's prediction of a second round win was going to hold.

In the second round it looked for a time that Mendes had McGregor in   real trouble. The experienced wrestler took him down and inflicted some damage. But McGregor's ground game was more developed than his critics had given him credit for.

Fatally, rather than continuing to do what he was doing and grinding McGregor down, Mendes gambled and went for a submission. The move failed and with both men back on their feet, and Mendes tired, McGregor moved in for the kill. Unleashing a series of uppercuts and body kicks, McGregor began his onslaught. McGregor fired in a powerful left cross and a few seconds later the referee stepped in and stopped the fight with just three seconds left in the round.

Mystic Mac's record was intact. He had stopped Mendes in the second round. McGregor was now the interim featherweight world champion amid jubilant scenes. His face streaked with blood from Mendes pounding his face while he was on the ground, McGregor was emotional as he celebrated with his family and support team.

In some ways it seems like the completion of a long journey. But Aldo was still out there, a human question that was still to be answered.

A KING IS CROWNED

The build-up to the fight with Jose Aldo, a fight that would settle who ended the night as the undisputed UFC featherweight champion appeared lower key than the hype surrounding their original scheduled meeting. Perhaps in terms of verbal sparring both men were a little punched out and fatigued from the previous world press tour.

McGregor certainly seemed much more relaxed. He said as much at the pre-fight press conference. He described himself as being in a state of zen, and there was no question that he appeared to exude more calmness and less of the manic energy than had been present before when he and Aldo were traveling the world to sell the first fight.

Perhaps his calm stemmed from now having in his possession a belt he coveted for so long. Or maybe he was simply relieved that Aldo has actually shown up ready to fight. Either way, McGregor's mood was different.

At the weigh in, he entered to a raucous atmosphere that was even louder than the weigh in for his fight with Mendes. The reaction of the crowd was like nothing the UFC has seen before. McGregor was cheered to the rafters while Aldo was relentlessly booed. The Irish were here again, there numbers even greater than before.

The fight itself, as described in greater detail in the opening chapter, was not what anyone has expected. Apart of course from McGregor who had outlined in detail ahead of time how he thought it would go. At the post-fight press conference he reminded a reporter of a discussion they had before the fight.

The reporter read back precisely what McGregor had said to him before the fight. "I felt when we stared down, I felt his right hand was twitching, which was a subtle tell for me. He is ready to unload that right hand and I feel that could be a downfall for him. If he lets that right hand go, I simply will not be there. I simply enter the way I enter, and that is enough. They either over-extend, or shrink away, but either way it is not good for them. I will create traps and dead space inside that Octagon and I will walk him into that dead space where all of a sudden he will be in danger."

While the Mystic Mac tag made for good copy, what became clear was the extent to which McGregor and Kavanagh studied his opponents. Attention to detail was critical. While McGregor's style was often called unpredictable by those he fought, many of them lacked that advantage. They tended to have a signature style that made them predictable. And in MMA fighting, predictability was dangerous.

With the victory against Aldo secured, McGregor was now the undisputed UFC featherweight champion. 2015 hadn't been without its surprises and challenges, but when all was said and done, it had been the year of McGregor. He had made good on his promises. What he had visualised as a destiny had come to pass.

In the process he had taken the UFC to new heights, drawing in people who had previously been indifferent to MMA. The evidence was there in the ticket sales and pay-per-view buys. In America the bottom line ruled, and McGregor made a big difference to the UFC's bottom line.

Now he had scaled the heights that he'd visualised the inevitable question was what next? For McGregor the answer was obvious. He wanted to reign as champion in more than one weight division, as he had done in his pre-UFC career when he had held both the featherweight and lightweight belts in the CWFC promotion.

Normally a champion would be expected to defend his existing belt, but the UFC was willing to accommodate McGregor's request. Their agreement stemmed not just from McGregor's bankability, but also from his willingness to fight regularly.

As Dana White had observed, what fighters say in public about wanting to take a match, and what they said in private were often two different things. Once fighters had made the climb and were financially more secure their motivation often ebbed away.

That was not going to be the case with McGregor.

THE REVERSAL

Great stories rely on twists, on the unexpected turn that when regarded in retrospect proves surprising yet somehow inevitable. So far McGregor's time in the UFC had been a linear narrative. He came, he fought, he won, he cashed the cheque. There were moments in some contests, most notably against Chad Mendes, when it appeared that he might come unstuck, but he hadn't.

Fueled by his public pronouncements and trash talk there was an eagerness among many fans of MMA, as well as many outside the sport, to see McGregor fail. It was palpable before every fight. There was also a sense that his supreme self-confidence was at risk of mutating into hubris. In many ways it was an unfair charge to level.

While McGregor's verbal onslaught against opponents before a fight was relentless, it did not carry on beyond the contest. The hallmark of his post-fight comments inside the Octagon in the immediate aftermath was the respect he showed to the other fighter.

Yet the idea that McGregor had become arrogant gained ground. Rather than shy away from it, McGregor played up to it. He made much of his new found wealth. He jabbed back at men he'd already beaten who challenged his credentials. He was not a champion given to turning the other cheek when he was attacked.

The media, even in Ireland, became more

critical. Now he was being criticised for the exact same qualities he had been lauded for only a short time ago. It was a classic reaction to success. There are few things newspapers enjoy more than building someone up only to tear them back down again.

McGregor mostly shrugged it off, and focused on his next fight. To the chagrin of other fighters in the weight division where he was champion, he lobbied to move up to lightweight. In the UFC's history two fighters had held belts at two different weight divisions, but none had done so simultaneously. McGregor wanted to be the first. Having become champion, and made millions of dollars in the process, now it was about cementing his place in history and building a legacy.

A fight was scheduled for the 5th of March, 2016. McGregor would fight the reigning lightweight champion Rafael Dos Anjos. Moving up a division against Do Anjos was seen as a gamble. Few fighters move up so quickly. They tend to defend their title where they are, at least for a time.

But McGregor was impatient. He felt that he had proven himself at featherweight. He wanted a fresh challenge, and Dos Anjos would certainly offer that. Which wasn't to say that in the first pre-fight press conference he offered the other champion any great measure of respect. In fact he went straight back to his trash talk play book in a bid to unsettle Dos Anjos.

This time the pressure point McGregor selected was the fact that Brazilian Dos Anjos, unlike his compatriot Jose Aldo, had settled in America. McGregor contrasted his own patriotism, and decision to remain based in Ireland, with his opponent's abandonment of Brazil. He even went as far as questioning Dos Anjos' decision to call his two sons Bob and Donald. For good or ill, it was classic McGregor. It drew laughs from the media and upset Dos Anjos.

As was now the pattern with McGregor's fights, on the 23rd of February, news broke that Dos Anjos had withdrawn from the fight with a broken left foot. Needless to say, alongside the disappointment and frustration, many were sceptical about whether the injury was the real reason behind Dos Anjos' withdrawal.

For the fourth time in eight fights, McGregor's opponent had pulled out at short notice. Injuries are not uncommon in MMA, but McGregor's opponents seemed to be remarkably unlucky. But McGregor himself was still game and the UFC went looking for a replacement. Having lobbied hard for a re-match, Jose Aldo turned down the chance to step back into the Octagon with McGregor, as did a number of other fighters. Finally, they turned to a fighter who rarely had a problem showing up.

Nate Diaz, brother of UFC fighter, Nick, was prepared to step up to the plate at extremely short notice. Although he didn't have the profile that McGregor had outside the sport, Diaz was a real character. A foul-mouthed trash talker he was also a formidable opponent with tremendous range, power and technique.

The Diaz brothers had grown up in the Northern Californian city of Stockton. A proudly working class place, Stockton is home to the largest inland seaport in the State of California. The Diaz brothers had a tough upbringing in a tough city where it would have been easy for them to fall into a life of crime.

Instead they had turned to martial arts and boxing. All the same, they remained products of their environment. Fiercely loyal to each other and their hometown, their relationship with the UFC had been turbulent at times. Unlike McGregor, neither brother played the game with Dana White and the UFC organisation. They were difficult to manage, petulant at times, and convinced, not without reason, that they hadn't reaped the rewards from the fight game that they were entitled to.

By taking the match with McGregor, Nate Diaz had the chance not only to make a huge payday, but also to upset what he and his brother saw as the UFC establishment. If McGregor was the UFC's golden boy, Nate Diaz was the black sheep of the family.

The decision was also made, in part because of the short notice, that the two men would fight at 170lbs. Bear in mind that McGregor held the belt at 145lbs, and he had been scheduled to fight Dos Anjos at 155lbs. The gap between a fighter's so called walking around weight and his fighting weight is bridged in the lead up to a fight by cutting, which involves an extreme diet, exercise and both excessive hydration followed by sudden dehydration. Part of McGregor's success lay in his ability to cut weight in an extremely efficient manner. To fight at 170lbs was a decision that many fans and commentators called into question.

Perhaps for the first time in his UFC career, McGregor also faced a challenger who was genuinely oblivious to psychological warfare. Diaz could talk trash with the best of them. He didn't have to appear to be a tough guy. He was a tough guy.

At one pre-fight press conference for UFC 197, the two men faced each other. Verbally, McGregor was in top form. Talking about his opponent, he said, "How can you not like him? He's like a little cholo gangster from the 'hood, but at the same time he coaches kids jiu-jitsu on a Sunday morning, and goes on bike rides with the elderly. He makes gun signs with the right hand and animal balloons with the left hand."

Diaz's pithy response ("Fuck you. Fuck your belt. I don't give a fuck what you think, motherfucker.") may not have been as witty as McGregor's salvo, but it was certainly direct and to the point. Importantly, Diaz's body language didn't betray the level of agitation that McGregor's verbal onslaughts usually drew from his opponent.

As McGregor started to respond to a question, Diaz lifted his microphone and lobbed a hand grenade, suddenly announcing, apropos of nothing, "They're all on steroids. They're all on steroids."

McGregor's head snapped round. It was his turn to be riled. "Steroids? What are you talking about, steroids?" McGregor, usually so perfectly in control at these events, and the one doing the prodding, was irritated. He quickly settled back into his rhythm but at least for a moment Diaz seemed to have gotten to him.

Underneath the verbal volleys it was also clear that their was genuine respect for each other. While the media played up their differences, in fact the two men had much in common, both in terms of their steely attitude, dedication to their craft, and aggressive fighting style. They were, as Diaz recognised in an interview he gave about McGregor before they were matched up, essentially kindred spirits.

Going into the day of the fight, McGregor was favourite, something which veteran fans found hard to believe given the jump in weight and Diaz's abilities. The expectation was that the McGregor bandwagon would keep on rolling, right over Nate Diaz. Diaz however had different plans. He planned on derailing the McGregor express.

Mystic Mac had predicted that he would stop Diaz near the end of the first round. And indeed, with another record crowd cheering him on, he did win the first round on points.

Going into the second McGregor seemed to be on course for another win. Diaz's face was bloodied and McGregor was landing punches. But the momentum changed when Diaz landed a big left hand that seems to rock McGregor back. Diaz pushed him against the fence and delivered another series of shots.

Later, McGregor would confess that he had started to panic. His blows, which would usually finish an opponent, were not having the same effect on the larger Diaz.

McGregor at this point was also struggling with his energy levels and breathing. He launched himself at Diaz and took the fight onto the floor. It was the beginning of the end for him. Diaz used his considerable wrestling and BJJ skills against him. Eventually Diaz placed McGregor in the dreaded rear naked choke hold. It's a hold that once applied is virtually impossible to escape from. The end result of a rear naked choke is unconsciousness.

McGregor tapped out, indicating his submission. The fight was over. Diaz had won. It was a major upset for many of McGregor's fans who were only used to seeing him win. The winning streak had come to an end.

In many ways what followed this defeat was not what many people would have expected. Rather than being humiliated, with his reputation damaged, his stature after the loss to Diaz only grew. In defeat, McGregor demonstrated humility and showed a side of himself that earned the respect of even his greatest critics.

THE AFTERMATH

Dramatists. novelists and screenwriters know that character hinges up action. How a person acts, or reacts, in a certain situation is revealing. It defines how they are perceived, but more importantly, it tells us who they are.

McGregor's attitude to defeat was one of gracious acceptance. He didn't try to make excuses. He didn't query his own decision making in taking on Diaz at a much greater weight. He accepted, he analyzed, and he gave credit to his opponent. The phrase he used to sum it up: "Humble in victory, and humble in defeat."

It was a reaction that won him new admirers, even among those who had criticised his brash approach. His capacity for self-examination in the moments immediately after the fight was striking. Talking to UFC commentator Joe Rogan, McGregor told him: "I took a chance, I gave up weight. It didn't work out. It is what it is. I'll face it like a man, like a champion, and come back and do it again."

McGregor also fulfilled his media obligations after the fight. A difficult task to perform in the immediate aftermath, and something that not every fighter does. He may have been beaten inside the Octagon, but he didn't slink away into a corner or hide. His answers were measured and analytical.

Talking to MMA reporter Ariel Helwani, Helwani asked a bruised and battered McGregor to describe his emotions. While his disappointment was plain to see, McGregor didn't flinch from the question. "It stings. It stings real bad. But this is the fight business. I've been on the end of many defeats in my life and I've always rose back, so I'll not shy away from it. I'll not make excuses for it. I'll assess it, and come back."

Needless to say online, in the world of social media, some of the McGregor haters were having a field day. And not just the fans either. Fighters who had declined the opportunity to take him on instead of Diaz were suddenly very vocal in calling him out. McGregor quite correctly questioned the character of men who had declined to fight him then taunting him because he had been beaten by someone who had taken the fight.

Perhaps McGregor's greatest external asset at this time was his coach, John Kavanagh, and in particular Kavanagh's philosophy. From the earliest days of Straight Blast Gym, Kavanagh had made a point of drilling into his young fighters that there were two outcomes to a fight: "Win or Learn". Indeed, it's the title of his upcoming autobiography (co-authored with the excellent Paul Dollery), which will be released at the end of June, and will surely be a must-read for anyone interested not just in MMA or McGregor, but coaching in general.

Kavanagh's influence is clear in McGregor's comments, and mature response, after the Diaz fight. What you take from a loss is in many ways more important than what you take from a win. Insightfully, Kavanagh also noted that in MMA, compared to say football, because fighters compete months apart, their losses are often overblown. Fighters lose. Even the best. Unexpected losses, or evenly-matched contests, are a testament to the health of MMA as a sport.

As long as he kept fighting regularly, the law of averages tells us that McGregor was bound to experience a loss. The question now was what would his next move be?

The answer, a rematch with Nate Diaz at UFC 200 in July of this year, was not what most people expected. If the original match up with Diaz at 170 was seen as risky, going back to take him on at the same weight, with Diaz having proper notice, seems to many to be reckless.

It was a decision originally opposed by the UFC who would have preferred to see McGregor drop back down to featherweight to defend his title. Understandably however, McGregor wants to exorcise this particular ghost.

The bookmakers have the contest dead even. Again it's a choice by McGregor that reveals much about his character. On paper it's hard to see anything other than another win for Nate Diaz. But what the defeat has given McGregor is a renewed focus and will to win.

If he does avenge the defeat by the Stockton fighter, his stock will soar to new heights. If he doesn't, his reputation will take a knock but he'll have many other options available. As with any decision that involves a large level of risk, if it comes off then you look smart. If it doesn't, you don't.

With that in mind, it's worth reminding people that McGregor has achieved what he has by taking risks. Most notably, he quit a solid apprenticeship when Ireland was in the midst of a crippling recession, and jobs were at a premium, to become a professional MMA fighter.

His career before the UFC came calling had defeats. Since then he has never shied away from a fight or an opponent. Quite the reverse in fact. His life has been one of achievement built on sacrifice.

McGregor has taken the UFC to a new level both financially, and in terms of its public profile. He is fiercely loyal to his family, his team and his fans. When he does decide to walk away from the fight game, he will do so a very rich man.

In a relatively short space of time, he has dazzled, entertained, enraged and captivated people around the world. The world of MMA is better for him. Regardless of what happens next, Conor McGregor has more than earned his iconic status.

AFTERWORD

Writing about Conor McGregor has been an education. Through his story, I have gained a genuine respect for the sport of MMA, and the people who take part in it at all levels. It is not only physically demanding in a way that few other sports are, it offers that a level of mental challenge that its critics often fail to acknowledge. The range of fighting styles and permutations of movement within the cage are considerable. It's little wonder that it looks set to eclipse boxing as the most closely followed combat sport in the world.

The people, and there are many, who rail against MMA as being violent and brutal and not a sport at all, miss the point. To compete in MMA takes tremendous sacrifice. As in any full contact sport, there are risks, not the least of which is head trauma.

I would however place the risks that MMA carries against the many positives it offers. Especially at a time when we face a tidal wave of public health issues brought about by lack of exercise and bad diet. Diabetes, heart problems, cancer and other diseases related to poor diet and lack of exercise are already scything their way through the population bringing huge costs in treatment as well as misery for individuals and families.

When placed in a broader context, anything that gets people, particularly kids and teenagers, up and active is a good thing. They'll also be taught lessons about hard work, discipline and taking care of themselves that will carry them through life and have a lasting positive legacy.

There is also another element to the criticism of MMA that's worth addressing. Snobbery. The popularity of MMA among young working class men makes it a particular target for certain other elements in society while other full contact sports such as rugby get a pass. In a world where masculinity is seen as more vice than virtue it's a shame that a sport that channels male aggression in a positive manner is so vilified.

With or without Conor McGregor, MMA is worthy of our respect. But one thing is for sure, we should enjoy watching McGregor while he's still competing. When he's gone, we will all be poorer for his absence.

ABOUT THE AUTHOR

Sean Black grew up in Scotland. He has written the screenplays for many of Britain's best known TV dramas. In 2008 he wrote his debut novel, *Lockdown*, which features private security operative, Ryan Lock. The book sold at auction, as part of a three book deal, for a six figure sum. Since then the Ryan Lock books have featured on several bestseller charts around the world and have been translated into Dutch, French, German, Italian, Portuguese, Russian, Spanish, and Turkish.

To research his novels, Sean has trained as a bodyguard with former members of the Royal Military Police's elite Close Protection Unit, spent time inside Pelican Bay Supermax prison in California, gone on numerous ride-alongs with the Los Angeles Police Department, and ventured deep into the tunnels under Las Vegas to interview some of the city's homeless population.

As well as the Ryan Lock series, he also writes the award-nominated Byron Tibor series of thrillers, and co-authors a series of mysteries set in Malibu, California with New York Times Bestseller, Rebecca Cantrell.

CPSIA information can be obtained
at www.ICGtesting.com
Printed in the USA
BVHW03s1236010618
517871BV00001BA/247/P